The Possibility of Happy

Possibility Takes Movement

By Raven McGee and Anna Talyn

Studio Talyn

Copyright © 2025 by Anna Talyn

All rights reserved. No part of this book may be reproduced, stored in a retrieval system, or transmitted in any form or by any means - electronic, mechanical, photocopy, recording, or otherwise - without prior written permission of the publisher, except in the case of brief quotations used in critical articles or reviews.

The Possibility of Happy: Possibility Takes Movement
By Raven McGee & Anna Talyn

Published by Studio Talyn
ISBN: 979-8-9998209-4-5

This book is offered as a guide for reflection and possibility. It is not intended as a substitute for medical, psychological, or legal advice. Readers should seek qualified care when needed. The stories and practices shared are starting points, not prescriptions. Every person's journey is unique, take what helps, set down what does not.

Printed in the United States of America

First Edition: 2025

Foreword

This is a guide about movement. Not the perfect plan. Not the impossible leap. Just the next honest inch.

We wrote *The Possibility of Happy* after years of living these ideas out loud, testing them in messy days, and watching what worked for real people. Inside you will find stories, frameworks, and simple experiments you can try before the page cools. The point is not to master every detail. The point is to turn toward possibility and feel it land in your actual life.

Raven spent more than twenty years studying people and our existence. Together we spent hundreds of hours workshopping these theories, challenging them, and refining them before deciding what was ready to share. What you hold here is not just Raven's voice or mine, but the best of both, combined into something more than either of us could have created alone.

Raven passed away before we could bring this book fully into the world. I have finished it in her memory, with deep gratitude for the years we spent building it side by side. My hope is that her wisdom continues to ripple outward through these pages, changing lives the way she changed mine.

Table of Contents

Foreword	3
Understanding Possibility	7
PhysioFX	24
The "U" of Learning	31
Rubber Band Theory	38
Is Frustration Undermining Real Growth?	43
The Morning and Afternoon of Life	47
The Six Points of Ego	51
The Connections	54
Sacrifice vs. Giving	58
Emotions	62
High Performance Habits	70
Reprogramming the Junk	74
Nutrition and Movement	78
The Lifecycle of Learning and Growth	82
Reprogramming the Brain	84
Closing Reflections	89
Practical Recap / Quick Guide	91
Acknowledgments	92
Closing Note	93

About this guide

Think of this as a field manual you can carry. Short sections. Plain language. A few core models you will see again until they feel like muscle memory. Survival to Possibility to Reconstruction to Fulfillment.

What we promise

When you go to bed tonight, we want you to look up at the ceiling and see more possible futures than you did last night. Not because the world changed. Because you did. Because you moved one inch and felt something unlock.

What this is not

This is not a doctrine. It is not a contest. It will not ask you to pretend you are fine. It will ask you to pay attention to the signals your mind and body keep sending, and to act on them one step at a time. We speak in general directions, then invite you to test, adjust, and make it yours.

Disclaimers

This book is offered as a guide for reflection and possibility. It is not a substitute for professional medical, psychological, or legal advice. If you need support in those areas, please seek qualified care.

The ideas, stories, and practices shared here are starting points, not prescriptions. They are invitations to notice, to experiment, and to choose what resonates for your life. Every person's body, mind, and journey is different. Take what helps, set down what does not.

How the information came

These pages are distilled from live workshops, coaching, and the unglamorous hours in between. We learned by listening to people, not just talking at them. We learned by failing, correcting, and trying again. We learned that hearing is not the same as learning, and that learning only sticks when it meets lived experience.

Terminology

Possibility
When we use the word *possibility*, we mean the capacity for change, growth, or new direction. It is not about predicting the future or chasing perfection. Possibility is what opens when you take a step, however small, toward movement. It creates space for what you want and releases what you are holding, making room for something new to come into your life.

Happy
Happy here is not constant joy or unbroken bliss. It is the experience of alignment , when your actions, values, and choices move together enough to create peace, resilience, or fulfillment. Happiness is not a finish line. It is a practice, available in moments and built over time.

We use the intentionally imperfect grammar in the phrase *the possibility of happy* so it stands out as a feeling in the present, not a destination in the future.

Fulfillment
Fulfillment means living in a rhythm that sustains you. It is different from survival (getting by) or possibility (glimpsing the next step). Fulfillment is when the new structures you build begin to feel like life itself rather than effort.

Reprogramming
Reprogramming is the process of noticing old scripts , the messages we inherited from childhood, culture, or trauma , and choosing new ones that serve growth. It is not erasing the past but replacing what no longer helps with what does.

Overflow
Overflow means giving from a place of fullness rather than depletion. Love, service, and care are most sustainable when they flow from a well that has been filled, not from sacrifice that empties you.

Fear
Fear shows up in two ways. *Survival fear* is the body's response to immediate danger, and it keeps us safe. *Growth fear* rises in the face of the unknown, when change is ahead but not yet defined. In the context of this book, fear of the unknown is often a guidepost pointing toward possibility.

Results you can expect

Clarity about where you are on the path. A handful of practices that lower friction right away. A way to think about tension that turns it from enemy to signal. Rituals for energy and attention. Language for love that does not empty you. Choices that stack. Momentum that holds.

The roadblocks we name

Default settings that keep you stuck. Fear of change, and the quieter fear of no change. Culture that sells quick fixes. Old stories about what you owe and who you have to be. We will not argue politics or religion. We will focus on what you can do in your kitchen, at your desk, on your walk, with your people.

Myths we set down

Sacrifice is the price of love: Incorrect. Love given from emptiness breeds resentment. Give from overflow.
Big change requires big drama: Incorrect. Small steps compound.
Emotions are the problem: Incorrect. Emotions are tools. Learn the grip and they help you move.

The team behind the pages

We came to this work from different roads and a shared conviction: People are capable. Change is natural. Momentum is earned. We met while researching identity and biology, comparing notes from business, coaching, parenting, and the long work of becoming a person on purpose. At some point our cupboards were full of "isn'ts." We built something else.

How to use this

Start where you are. Pick one practice. Swap one habit. Try the morning juice if nights are heavy. Make lunch lighter and see what happens. Journal the stretch and the retraction so you stop mistaking growth for failure. Notice the pages when the universe seems to tap your shoulder. Follow one.

A last word before you begin

We could wake up to world peace every morning, then spend the day making a mess of it. So start smaller. Start kinder. Start now. If all you do today is move one inch toward the life that feels like yours, you are already in the work. Possibility takes movement. This is your first step.

Raven's Tale

Raven McGee's story was never just about survival. It was about paying attention to signals, inching forward when leaps weren't possible, and carrying those lessons into every space she touched.

She grew up shy, carrying both the weight of dyslexia and the quiet fear of standing apart. There are small, vivid memories: an Easter egg hunt where she couldn't step more than a dozen paces from her mother, a haunted house she couldn't bring herself to enter, a classroom where even speaking her name aloud felt impossible. Those early hesitations gave her an understanding of what fear feels like in the body, how it shrinks movement, and how much courage it takes to push through.

Baseball and softball became her first anchors. One Saturday morning, at eight years old, she was asked if she wanted to play. She ran onto the field and caught every ball thrown her way. From then on, she kept playing, through knee surgery, through setbacks, teaching herself how the body recovers and how discipline transforms weakness into strength. Music and rhythm joined the mix. Drumline, piano, coding, football: Raven collected skills the way some people collect lifelines, each one a system she could enter, master, and share.

Life tested her with tension and contradiction. She built a business career that placed her in Fortune 500 circles, yet carried the memory of being that quiet child on the margins. She studied how to fit in, then used what she learned to coach others who felt the same strain. Her coworkers noticed. One evening, a customer paused before leaving and said simply, "Hey, you made it through the day." The weight of that moment stayed with her. She realized that surviving visibly, without hiding the struggle, gave others permission to keep going.

There were family fractures too deep to ignore. Years of tension at home, shouting, manipulation, constant threats of leaving, forced Raven to turn her focus toward raising her son, Junior, with intention. She taught him love as a daily practice, singing to him in the car seat: *you love everyone because everyone loves you.* She repeated it until it became truth in his small body. Even in the hardest season, when her business and marriage were crumbling at once, she made that practice of love the anchor.

She let the store go in 2012, and with it, the old version of life. What remained was growth. She started writing, using her blog as catharsis and clarity. She committed to sobriety back in 1988, and decades later, she still pointed to that choice as one of the foundations of her freedom. She held deep talks with people since the mid-90s, often long before coaching was considered a profession. By 2010, she recognized what had been true all along: her focus belonged not just in business, but in coaching, teaching, and helping people see possibility.

Raven's story is one of practice. Like a doctor seeing patients, she treated each day as a chance to learn and to pass that learning forward. She believed we live the same life in different shapes, and that sharing the lessons of one could ease the path for another. Her tale doesn't end with hardship. It widens into community, teaching, and the steady conviction that possibility takes movement, one inch, one practice, one choice at a time.

In the years that followed, Raven found love again. She married, built a home grounded in the lessons she carried, and continued to mentor others with the same warmth and directness that had always marked her voice. When she passed away, she left more than memories. She left a framework for living, simple, practical, hopeful, that still moves through the people she touched. Her life remains a signal worth noticing, a reminder that survival is only the beginning, and that fulfillment is found in how we love, how we teach, and how we keep choosing possibility.

Anna's Tale

Anna Talyn grew up in a small Central Minnesotan town, the kind of place where family names carried weight and routine shaped everything. It was a German-Catholic community, tucked beside a nuclear power plant on the Mississippi. The backdrop was ordinary, but her early years were marked by a quiet, steady resistance to becoming ordinary herself.

As a child she was shy, shaped by a mother's severe anxiety and her own instinct to hide. On days when she missed school, she kept her head low in the car whenever someone passed by, worried they might question why she wasn't in class. Even then she was observing systems, how they worked, how fear could stall them, and how one small act of courage could reset them.

Courage showed itself in flashes. She fought for her right to play on the playground, even when the bully was twice her size. She mediated between classmates, talking them out of fights. In middle school she stood up to a kickboxer who bullied others, proving to herself that fear didn't have to be the last word. She pushed through the noise of adolescence and began to recognize that systems could be changed if someone was willing to disrupt them.

Her father was her hero. From him she learned the shape of strength and the belief that becoming who you needed to be was possible, even when it took more than you thought you had. By eighth grade, when her mother went into the hospital, Anna carried that lesson forward: systems break, but they can also be repaired.

High school widened the lens. She was still a misfit, voted most shy in her grade, but she carried diverse interests, bouncing between shop class, English, media production, and work programs. She found independence in small ways: buying her first car, later saving every penny to purchase clothes and lunches on her own. Those choices became early proof of character.

There were moments of grace threaded through hardship. As a senior, she began dating a girl who had survived a devastating accident. Partially paraplegic at the time, her girlfriend fought her way back to walking. Anna saw firsthand that survival and change were not just theories. They lived in bodies, in effort, in the long days of not giving up.

Work became her constant. She carried a reputation of being "very straight-laced," pushing herself through long hours, even round-the-clock schedules. Her pattern was clear: if there was something she wanted, she would make it happen, even if fear stood in the way. When she bought her dream car, the person who helped her secure it was the very bully she had once feared most. It was a reminder that power shifts, and that persistence outlasts intimidation.

Life tested her with cycles of building and breaking. She left an abusive job and launched her own business, only to face foreclosure and bankruptcy. She started again at a radiology company with a beat-up car, clawing her way into a new beginning. She and her spouse battled through six painful years trying to have children, enduring miscarriages, spending savings, holding on through grief. The arrival of her daughter was a turning point. Holding her for the first time gave Anna the strength to live authentically, no matter the cost.

She carried that conviction through another storm: nearly divorcing on a trip, holding out on living fully until after her son was born, then convincing her spouse to pack up their life, two babies, two cats, one fragile hope, and move across the country. The marriage did not survive those transitions, but Anna did. She lost nearly everything, fell in love for the first time only to lose again, and still kept moving forward. Each loss became proof that starting over was not the end.

By the time she met Raven McGee, she was already practiced building from ruins. The two began to work together, combining voices, stories, and frameworks into something neither could have made alone. For Anna, it was the beginning of fully embracing her purpose.

Her story does not end in survival either. By 2024 she had found love again, engaged to be married, and still carrying the same conviction that has defined her path: possibility is not a gift you wait for. It is built choice by choice, setback by setback, new beginning by new beginning. Anna never let starting over deter her. She turned it into her practice. Into her Possibility of Happy.

Understanding Possibility

The How, Definitions, and Theories

Next Necessary Movement

Possibility is not a destination waiting at the far end of the road. It is movement itself. Each step you take, no matter how small, is what turns potential into lived change. You cannot skip ahead. If you try to leap over the early stages, you risk building on air. Foundations matter.

Think of it like building a house. If you pour concrete without framing, or try to put on the roof before the walls, the whole thing collapses. Change works the same way. Survival has to stabilize before Possibility can appear. Reconstruction has to be practiced before Fulfillment can hold. Skipping steps feels tempting. We all want the fast ending, but those shortcuts usually topple.

Don't Jump to the End

The end will come in its own time. Rushing there does not make it arrive faster. It only makes the ground less steady beneath you. You may imagine what the finished picture will look like, a healthier body, a stronger relationship, a calmer mind, but the real work is in the scaffolding. In choosing what comes next today.

Don't Worry About How It Ends Up

The truth is you do not know where it will end. That is not failure. That is freedom. It could be good. It could even be great. The point is not to predict the exact outcome but to stay in the process. Possibility is about journey, not arrival. Every step reshapes the ending anyway.

The Pillars

Everyone leans on pillars. Some are obvious: routines, relationships, beliefs. Others are quieter, like unspoken habits that make you feel safe. When change begins, those pillars can feel threatened. Honoring them matters. If you take one away, you may need to build another that serves the same function. A substitute pillar is not weakness. It is scaffolding until new strength grows.

The aim is not to tear your structure apart. It is to adjust the function while keeping stability. Without that respect, people may collapse under change rather than move through it.

Purpose

Purpose is not optional. It is the engine that keeps you moving when the early excitement wears off and resistance shows up. Without purpose, every step feels heavier. With it, even setbacks become part of the rhythm. Purpose does not have to be grand. It has to be true enough to matter when it is hard.

How to Smile

In this process, the smile is not the starting point. It is the sign that the work has settled inside you. A knowing smile arrives at the end, when the pieces fit enough for you to trust yourself again. It is not forced optimism or a mask to cover pain. It is the quiet curve of recognition: *I made it further this time. I can keep going.*

Reflection and Practice

1. **Notice.** Think about the last time you tried to skip ahead in a process. What happened when you rushed?

2. **Assess.** What pillars keep you steady right now: routines, relationships, or habits? Which ones feel shaky?

3. **Act.** Choose one step you can take today, no matter how small, to reinforce your foundation instead of chasing the finish line.

Example

A new teacher steps into her first classroom. On the first day she imagines herself as an expert already, skipping ahead to the polished picture in her head. But when the noise builds and the lesson plan falls apart, she realizes foundations come first: learning the students' names, setting routines, and creating trust. The work feels slower than she hoped, yet those small steps keep the whole structure from toppling. Possibility is not in rushing to mastery. It is in building the ground steady enough to hold it.

Survival to Fulfilment

There are two common ways people measure success. One is by money. The other is not.

The money path is defined by what you have, how much you can buy, and what others think of you. The other path is defined by togetherness and family, by the quality of daily life, and by what you carry inside. Rules, laws, school curriculums, inflation, even detention, these structures shape the outside, but fulfillment grows inside. Struggles double when loved ones are hurting too, and families often fall into cycles of bickering in every direction.

Survival to fulfillment is a process. You start with survival, getting through the day, covering the basics, holding on. Possibility enters when you glimpse that life could be more than endurance. Reconstruction is the work of rebuilding habits, relationships, and systems. Fulfillment happens when those new structures hold long enough to feel like life instead of effort.

At times the shift is almost visible. A thought catches you. A memory rises. A puzzle is solved not by you alone but with someone's help. Warmth grows into appreciation, respect, and love. Tears are not a sign of failure but of recognition. They signal that you touched something true. A family gathered, a holiday scene, even a handful of bubbles rising into the air can hold that reminder. When logic and emotion finally meet, possibility is no longer a theory. It is a feeling you can touch.

Keep it simple. It can be Sally or Sam, the ordinary person in your life who proves the extraordinary just by showing up.

The nuance is in the motive. Ask yourself: am I doing this for me or for them? If the balance leans toward yourself, it can be ego. If the balance leans toward another, it can be diligence. Fulfillment often comes when the scale steadies between the two.

Example

A couple facing financial strain spends months only in survival , paying bills late, arguing, trying to stretch groceries. Possibility begins when one of them takes a free online course and sees that another future might exist. Reconstruction follows with late nights of budgeting, new habits, and steady discipline. Fulfilment shows up when bills are current and dinners include laughter again. The same house feels different because the energy is no longer only about enduring.

Example: Survival to Fulfilment in a Relationship

Survival. Dinner was quiet. Words had become sparks waiting to catch, so both stayed silent. Every conversation felt like walking across glass. They weren't living together so much as getting through the same days under one roof.

Possibility. One night, something small broke the silence. A clumsy bump in the kitchen. A shared look at the same moment. Then laughter, surprising, shaky, but real. For the first time in months, they remembered what it felt like to like each other. That laugh was not a fix. It was a glimpse.

Reconstruction. They began trying again, awkwardly at first. She paused before snapping back. He learned to circle back with softer words. They both practiced small repairs, even when pride wanted to win. Some nights still ended in slammed doors, but the rhythm shifted. Habits slowly bent toward healing.

Fulfilment. Months later, the house felt lighter. They still argued, but they also found their way back to each other quicker. A hand offered in the middle of a fight. An apology spoken without prompting. Trust grew in layers. Fulfilment wasn't perfection. It was the return of ease. Home no longer felt like a place to endure. It felt like a place to rest.

Reflection and Practice

1. **Notice.** Where are you right now: survival, possibility, reconstruction, or fulfillment? Write it honestly.

2. **Assess.** Think about your motive. Are you acting from ego or diligence? Where does the balance lean?

3. **Act.** Take one step this week that moves you one stage further, even if it is as small as asking for help or naming gratitude aloud.

Modality

Change is inevitable. Change is natural. Stasis is an illusion. Control is an illusion. Perfection is not attainable and should never be the goal. What matters most is the direction you choose.

Growing or retreating are the two modalities of change. You are either leaning into growth, however small the step, or you are pulling back. Retreat is not failure. It is a pause, a lesson, a retraction before the next stretch. Growth, even painful growth, signals life.

One way to recognize the shift is to notice your happy place. The point is not to escape there but to bring the feelings from that space into the world you actually live in. In your dreams you should always be the hero. It should always work out. That truth is not fantasy. It is practice.

Recognizing possibility works the same way. The smile is not the beginning of the process. It is the sign that the work has taken root. Possibility already exists where you are today. It is not a future prize. It is a daily reality. When you notice a genuine smile breaking through, not forced and not for show, it is an early indicator that possibility is moving in you.

Our role is to help you recognize and act on it. To find where you are now, to clarify where you want to go, and to map the steps between. That work begins with goals. Write them. Name them. If you were in a workshop with us, we might ask you to post them publicly to create accountability, then return later to compare how far you have come.

What matters is not the platform or the proof. What matters is the practice. Each choice, each goal, each smile is another step in the movement from survival to fulfillment.

Example

A young nurse feels the weight of burnout. Growing means learning to set boundaries, taking breaks, asking for support. Retreating means ignoring her body's signals and slipping further into exhaustion. Both choices are real. Only one sustains. Growth in her case is not dramatic. It is leaving work on time twice a week and taking walks before bed. Those small choices begin to restore the rhythm of life.

Reflection and Practice

1. **Notice.** Are you currently growing or retreating? No judgment, just observe.

2. **Assess.** What is your "happy place", and what feelings live there?

3. **Act.** Bring one of those feelings into your present world. If peace lives there, find a way to carry peace into today's routine.

Do You Like Yourself?

This is where possibility begins to turn inward. You can set goals, build systems, and practice new habits, but if underneath it all you cannot stand the person you see in the mirror, the foundation cracks.

Liking yourself is not vanity. It is the ability to sit with your own company without constant distraction. It is the quiet trust that you are worth the effort of change.

Do You Accept Yourself?

Acceptance is different from liking. Liking yourself might come and go with mood or circumstance. Acceptance is deeper. It is the steady agreement to live in your own skin, to honor the story you carry, and to stop fighting the fact that you are here.

You do not have to love every detail of your past to accept yourself in the present. Acceptance means you stop treating your own life as a problem to solve and start treating it as a place to grow.

Example

For years a man avoided mirrors, brushing his teeth without looking up. One day he forces himself to glance, then slowly begins to meet his own eyes. It is uncomfortable at first, but over time the habit shifts. Acceptance arrives not as liking every detail but as no longer hiding from himself. The reflection becomes less enemy and more companion.

Reflection and Practice

1. **Notice.** Are you currently growing or retreating? No judgment, just observe.

2. **Assess.** What is your "happy place", and what feelings live there?

3. **Act.** Bring one of those feelings into your present world. If peace lives there, find a way to carry peace into today's routine.

Your Choices, Mistakes, Accomplishments

Every life is a mixture of these three. Choices you made, mistakes you regret, accomplishments you are proud of. The balance shifts depending on the day you look back.

Possibility comes when you can hold all three without losing yourself in any one of them. Choices are not permanent sentences. Mistakes are not final verdicts. Accomplishments are not your only worth. Together they make a whole life, and that life can change direction at any point.

The Power of Loving Yourself

Loving yourself is not selfish. It is survival. When you learn to extend compassion inward, you create overflow that can extend outward. Without it, giving becomes depletion. With it, giving becomes multiplication.

Loving yourself means acknowledging the full picture:choices, mistakes, accomplishments, and still deciding you are worthy of care, worthy of effort, worthy of possibility.

Example

A mother used to run herself ragged, believing love meant never resting. Eventually she began taking short naps while her children read beside her. Instead of losing love, she noticed her children copying her, curling up with books, learning rest without guilt. Loving herself did not take from them. It multiplied outward.

Reflection and Practice

1. **Notice.** How do you usually treat yourself when you fall short?

2. **Assess.** What message would you give a close friend in the same situation? Compare it to what you told yourself.

3. **Act.** Replace one harsh inner response this week with a gentler one, spoken as if you were talking to someone you love.

Levels of Understanding Your Daily Perspective

1. **Able to function day to day (stable).** You can meet basic needs and responsibilities, even if deeper fulfillment feels far away.

2. **Loving others without controlling.** You let people be who they are without bending them to fit your needs.

3. **Being loved without being controlled.** You allow love in without surrendering your agency or identity.

4. **Forgiveness.** You stop carrying the weight of past harm, whether from yourself or others. Forgiveness does not erase the past. It lightens the hold it has on your future.

Example

Level 1. A man drags himself through the workday, steady enough to function but with no space for more.

Level 2. A woman listens to her friend cry without rushing to fix it, showing love without control.

Level 3. A partner allows affection in without suspicion, learning to be loved without being controlled.

Level 4. Two sisters meet after years of silence, forgiveness softening what anger once held.

Reflection and Practice

1. **Notice.** Which level describes you right now: stable function, loving without controlling, being loved without control, or forgiveness?

2. **Assess.** Where do you most often get stuck?

3. **Act.** Choose one practice to move one level deeper, let someone be themselves without correction, or release one old grudge that still drains you.

PhysioFX

PhysioFX is the name we use for the interaction between your body, your brain, and your community. It is short for *physiological effects*. Every thought, every choice, and every connection creates a response in your body. Those responses, in turn, shape how you think, how you act, and how you show up for others.

PhysioFX reminds us that emotions live in the body first. Anxiety can tighten the chest. Depression can slow digestion. Gratitude can relax muscles. Laughter can release endorphins. What you feel is never separate from what your body carries.

Learning to listen to those signals: hunger, tension, fatigue, energy, is essential. They are not distractions. They are guides.

PhysioFX is not a single solution. It is a framework. It shows how biology, psychology, and community weave together, and how you can use that awareness to create more possibility in daily life. It begins with noticing how you currently meet your needs and experimenting with healthier, more sustainable options. Each adjustment creates ripples, and those ripples form the waves of change.

Brain

The brain is the central processor. It builds shortcuts, patterns, and default settings so you can move through the world quickly. This efficiency is useful, but it can also lock you into habits that no longer serve you. Stress, fear, and old programming become loops that keep you stuck in survival mode.

Recognizing your brain's tendency toward shortcuts is the first step in reprogramming. Awareness gives you the choice to stop reacting out of habit and start responding with intention.

Community

No one lives in isolation. Your physiology is affected by the people around you. Stress spreads. Calm spreads. Encouragement builds resilience, while constant criticism tears it down.

Community shapes what your brain accepts as normal. If you surround yourself with people committed to growth, your body and mind will align with that rhythm. If you stay in circles defined by fear or scarcity, your system adapts to that instead.

Nutrition

What you eat changes how you think and feel. Heavy foods can slow the body and cloud the mind. Lighter, nutrient-dense foods often create more clarity and energy. Balance matters more than extremes. A pattern of nourishment creates space for possibility, while a pattern of depletion makes even small changes harder to sustain.

Exercise

Movement resets the system. It burns through stress hormones, increases circulation, and releases endorphins that elevate mood. Exercise does not have to mean marathons or gyms. Walking, stretching, or dancing in your living room are all forms of movement that remind your body it is alive, capable, and adaptable.

Six Human Needs

Every person is driven by the same six needs. The way we meet them differs, but the pull is universal.

1. **Certainty.** A sense of safety and stability.
2. **Variety.** A break from routine, stimulation, surprise.
3. **Love and Connection.** Belonging, intimacy, and shared care.
4. **Significance.** Knowing you matter, that your life carries weight.
5. **Growth.** Expanding skills, awareness, and capacity.
6. **Contribution.** Giving beyond yourself, leaving the world better than you found it.

When these needs are met in healthy ways, the body and mind work in harmony. When they are met in destructive ways, through control, addiction, or empty distractions, the system strains.

Example

A man volunteers at a neighborhood food shelf. Certainty comes from the routine of showing up every Saturday. Variety shows up in the stories he hears from strangers. Love and connection grow as faces become familiar. Significance rises when he realizes others count on him. Growth comes through new skills in organizing and outreach. Contribution speaks for itself , giving beyond himself makes the world better than he found it.

Example: A Day in PhysioFX

Imagine a person walking into work already carrying stress.

- **Brain.** Their thoughts loop around unfinished tasks. The brain defaults to survival mode, scanning for problems rather than solutions.

- **Body.** Shoulders tighten, digestion slows, and fatigue sets in before the day begins. The body translates mental stress into physical strain.

- **Community.** In the office, tension spreads. Conversations feel shorter, coworkers respond with guarded energy, and the whole group picks up on the undercurrent.

- **Nutrition and Exercise.** Lunch is fast food eaten at the desk. No walk, no break, no reset. The system stays heavy and fogged.

- **Six Needs.** Certainty is shaken by job insecurity. Variety is reduced to interruptions and distractions. Love and connection feel thin. Significance is questioned. Growth feels stalled. Contribution fades under the weight of simply getting through.

Now imagine one small adjustment. That same person takes a ten-minute walk after lunch. Movement loosens the shoulders, resets circulation, and clears the mind. On return, a genuine smile shows up in conversation. That ripple changes how coworkers respond. Stress lightens. Community shifts. Certainty and connection begin to restore.

This is PhysioFX in action. The body, the brain, and the community interact constantly. Each choice, even a small one, creates ripples. Enough ripples build into waves, and those waves move you toward possibility.

Example

At a community yoga class, one person arrives tense and irritable. The room is calm, voices are quiet, movements slow. Within minutes their breathing deepens to match the group. By the end of class, stress has melted. Community shaped physiology, showing how quickly energy can shift when people share rhythm and intention.

Example: PhysioFX in Daily Life

Brain. He woke up already behind. The first thought was a list of what hadn't been done yesterday. By the time he poured coffee, his mind was sprinting, rehearsing problems before the day even began. The brain had chosen survival mode, scanning for threats instead of possibilities.

Body. Shoulders hunched tight by mid-morning. His stomach churned. Lunch was a fast grab from the vending machine , quick sugar, quick salt. It kept him moving, but the fog thickened. The body carried what the brain had rehearsed.

Community. At work, tension spread. His clipped answers made others defensive. Jokes fell flat. A coworker who had started the day calm walked away with a frown. Stress rippled outward, shaping the atmosphere around him.

Nutrition. By late afternoon he was dragging. He grabbed another soda, more caffeine, another short burst that would collapse within the hour. His body was asking for nourishment, but habit only delivered depletion.

Exercise. Normally he would drive straight home and collapse on the couch. That day, out of frustration more than inspiration, he chose a short walk instead. Ten minutes outside. Shoulders loosened. Breathing slowed. The fog lifted enough to see clearly.

Six Needs. In that simple walk, several of his human needs shifted. Certainty - the rhythm of his feet on pavement gave stability. Variety - fresh air and movement broke the cycle. Love and connection, a quick hello to a neighbor. Significance - pride in not giving up on himself. Growth - proof he could choose differently. Contribution - showing up at home calmer than before. It was only ten minutes. But those minutes changed his brain, his body, and his community. The ripple was visible.

Reflection and Practice

1. **Body Check.** Where do you feel stress in your body first: chest, stomach, shoulders, jaw?

2. **Needs Audit.**

    Which of the six human needs do you meet in **healthy** ways?

    - Certainty
    - Variety
    - Love and Connection
    - Significance.
    - Growth
    - Contribution

    Which ones are you meeting through habits that **drain** you?

    - Certainty
    - Variety
    - Love and Connection
    - Significance.
    - Growth
    - Contribution

3. **One Change.** Choose one small adjustment this week. Drink water instead of soda. Walk for five minutes after lunch. Call a friend instead of scrolling. Notice how that change ripples into your mood, your body, and your community. What one adjustment will you make this week?

The "U" of Learning

Raven described learning as a "U." The shape itself explains the journey. You begin high, slide down into challenge, and only rise again by moving through choice and change. Each part of the U adds a layer of understanding that cannot be skipped.

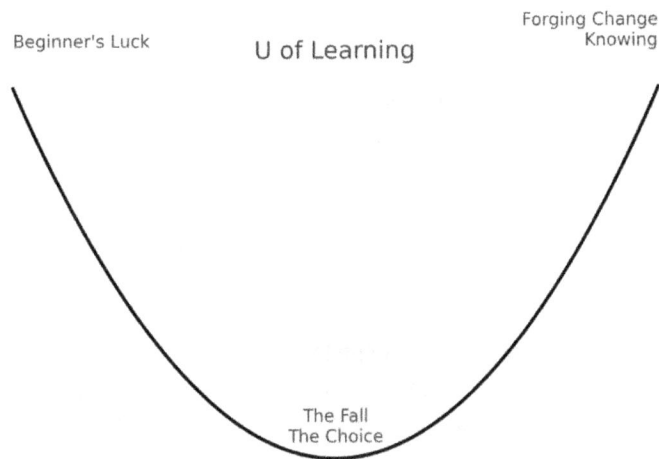

Beginner's Luck

At the top of the U, everything feels easy. You try something new and it works better than expected. Progress feels natural, even effortless. Beginner's luck is not a trick , it is a burst of possibility. It gives you just enough confidence to step in further. But that is not the whole story.

The Fall

Soon after comes the drop. What once felt easy now feels clumsy. The early wins fade. The gap between what you imagined and what you can actually do shows itself. This is where most people quit, assuming the ease at the start was the truth. The fall is not failure. It is part of the curve.

The Choice

At the bottom of the U, you face a decision. Do you stop here, or do you keep going? The choice is the hinge of the process. Quitting means losing the chance to rise. Continuing means accepting that learning takes effort, discipline, and time. The choice defines whether the U becomes a closed loop or a full journey.

Forging Change

If you choose to continue, the next stage is forging change. This is practice, repetition, and discomfort. It is showing up even when progress is invisible. It is the daily work of re-wiring the brain, strengthening the body, and shifting old patterns. Forging change feels heavy, but it is where deep learning actually happens.

The Arrival (Knowing)

On the far side of the U comes knowing. This is not the same as beginner's luck. It is steadier, rooted in experience. You understand not only how to do the thing but also what it means. Knowing carries both confidence and humility, confidence in your skill, humility from the process it took to get here.

The U of learning reminds us that falling is part of the shape, not the end of the story. The arrival only holds its weight because of the fall, the choice, and the forging in between.

Example 1: Learning Guitar

Beginner's Luck. A new player strums a few chords and learns a song in a week.

The Fall. Harder songs expose clumsy fingers and buzzing strings. Frustration builds.

The Choice. They decide whether to quit or keep practicing.

Forging Change. Daily ten-minute practice builds muscle memory and rhythm.

The Arrival. Months later, they no longer just press strings. They make music.

Example 2: Changing Nutrition

Beginner's Luck. Someone decides to cut back on sugar. The first week they feel lighter, energy spikes, and they imagine the whole process will be simple.

The Fall. Cravings kick in. Mood dips. Old habits call louder than expected. The first burst of energy fades and discouragement sets in.

The Choice. They stand at the bottom of the U: return to old patterns, or keep going? Choosing to continue means accepting that withdrawal, setbacks, and slow progress are part of the path.

Forging Change. They replace soda with sparkling water, pack fruit for work, and give themselves grace when they stumble. Small adjustments repeat until they begin to stick.

The Arrival. Weeks later, the cravings ease. They notice clarity in their thinking, steadier energy, and pride in their discipline. The change is no longer a temporary test. It is part of who they are.

Reflection and Practice

1. **Notice.** Think of an area of your life: skill, health, or relationship, where you started strong and then stalled.

2. **Assess.** Where are you on the U right now? Beginner's luck, the fall, the choice, forging change, or knowing?

3. **Act.** Decide one small practice you will keep, even if it feels invisible today. That practice is the bridge up the far side of the U.

Example: The U of Learning in Self-Talk

Beginner's Luck. After reading an inspiring book, she felt unstoppable. For the first few days she caught herself smiling in the mirror, convinced she could keep her mindset positive. The U began high.

The Fall. By the end of the week, the old voice crept back in. One mistake at work, one offhand comment from a friend, and the familiar chorus of *you're not enough* returned. The new positivity felt flimsy, like a coat of paint already cracking. This was the fall.

The Choice. At the bottom of the U she faced the decision. Should she drop the whole effort and accept that negative self-talk was just part of who she was, or should she keep practicing even when it felt fake? She chose to keep trying.

Forging Change. Day after day, she caught the harsh words mid-thought and replaced them with softer ones: *I messed up, but I'm learning. I'm tired, but I'm still moving forward.* At first it felt forced, like speaking a foreign language. Over time the words became less awkward. Repetition forged new grooves.

The Arrival. Months later she realized the shift when a mistake happened and the first thought wasn't attack but encouragement. The harsh voice still appeared, but it no longer ruled. She had moved from effort into knowing. This was not beginner's luck. It was the steady confidence of someone who had practiced their way into a new truth.

Reflection and Practice

1. **Notice.** What does your inner voice sound like when you make a mistake?

2. **Assess.** Where are you on the U of Learning with your self-talk, beginner's luck, the fall, the choice, forging change, or arrival?

3. **Act.** Choose one phrase of gentler self-talk you can use this week. Repeat it every time the old voice rises. Repetition is what carries you up the far side of the U.

Rubber Band Theory

A student once asked the Zen teacher Suzuki Roshi to reduce all of Buddhism to a single phrase. Suzuki laughed and replied, "Everything changes."

That simple truth is the ground of life. Change is constant. Growth is constant. The only illusion is that we can hold things still.

Yet humans complicate what is simple. Our brains are wired for efficiency. We create patterns, programs, and shortcuts so we can move through the world quickly. These patterns save energy, but they resist change. They make us believe we "know" things that are really only assumptions. Left unchecked, they can harden into bias, stereotypes, and habits that block growth.

Real growth asks us to rewrite those programs. To let go of what no longer works. To stretch into something new. And stretching, as anyone who has ever pulled on a rubber band knows, always creates tension.

That is the essence of Rubber Band Theory.

Stretch and Resistance

When you grow, you expand like a rubber band. You never return to the exact size you were before. Each stretch makes you larger, gives you new perspective, new potential.

But with expansion comes resistance. Old habits, old fears, old identities pull back. You feel the tension of retraction. This is why growth often feels like two steps forward and one step back. The key is to recognize that retraction is not failure. It is a natural part of the process. You are still bigger than you were.

If you expect only momentum, the pullback will discourage you. But if you understand the rubber band, you know that resistance is proof you have stretched.

Energy in the Stretch

In physics, momentum is a force. Something in motion tends to stay in motion. Change works the same way. When you stretch, you create potential energy. Even when you feel pulled back, that energy is still there, waiting to be released into possibility.

The question is not whether you will feel resistance. You will. The question is how you channel the energy of that resistance. Defeat, or possibility.

A Story from the Field

Years ago, I worked in the medical technology field during a period of rapid growth. My company had just merged with a competitor, doubling in size overnight. My role was to help the new combined team learn our systems. On paper it was training. In practice, it was something closer to life coaching.

The challenge was massive. The operations center was closing. Anyone unwilling to relocate from the desert warmth to a far colder state would lose their job. Stress was high, morale was low, and the future felt uncertain.

I introduced Rubber Band Theory to the team. I explained that the discomfort they felt was the tension of stretching, the old habits and roles pulling back against the new reality. But inside that tension was potential energy. If we stayed with it, we could turn struggle into momentum.

It worked. Out of forty people, only four left early. Six stayed on in extended support roles. A handful relocated. The rest moved forward with resilience. Many of them reframed the experience as growth, even using the merger on their resumes as proof they could adapt.

The process was painful, but the outcome was extraordinary. The team unified and achieved results no one in our industry had reached before. We created possibility out of struggle.

The Takeaway

If you are being stretched right now, remember this: the tension you feel is not proof you are failing. It is proof you are growing. The resistance is real, but so is the expansion. Each stretch makes you bigger than before. Each pullback still leaves you larger than you were.

You are filled with potential energy. The work is to aim it toward possibility.

Story: Rubber Band Theory

The first stretch came when she took the promotion. New title, new office, the kind of leap she had been waiting for. At first it felt expansive, like oxygen filling the room. She could almost feel herself growing into it.

Then came the pullback. The extra hours. The old doubts. The late nights staring at the ceiling, hearing the voice that said maybe she was in too far. Momentum turned heavy. The rubber band snapped taut.

Survival looked like coffee and calendar alerts. But under it all was the hum of tension, the ache of being stretched.

Weeks later, she noticed something small. A meeting that once rattled her now felt steadier. She spoke without shaking. She saw her team lean in when she did. The stretch had left a mark. Even as the band pulled back, she wasn't who she had been. She had grown wider. Stronger.

This is the rhythm no one tells you about. Expansion, resistance, retraction. Two steps forward, one back. The temptation is to call the pullback failure, to mistake tension for collapse. But the truth is she could never shrink to her original size. Each stretch stayed. Each retraction carried her further than before.

She still feels it today, that tight snap when growth asks for more. But now, instead of fear, she recognizes it as potential. The band is stretching again.

Reflection and Practice

1. **Notice.** Think about a time when you stretched yourself, a new job, a new habit, a difficult change. What resistance showed up as you expanded?

2. **Assess.** Did you interpret the pullback as failure, or did you see it as part of the process? How did that perspective shape your next step?

3. **Act.** Choose one area of life where you feel tension right now. Reframe it as potential energy, the rubber band being stretched. Write down one way you can aim that energy toward possibility instead of discouragement.

Is Frustration Undermining Real Growth?

Most people know the feeling. A team that should be thriving stalls. A project slows down despite good intentions. You wake up already bracing for the meeting ahead. Frustration is common, and it can quietly erode even the strongest organizations.

But frustration is not the enemy. At its core, frustration is simply the gap between what you expect and what you experience. Results do not line up with effort. Conversations do not match intentions. Progress lags behind vision. That gap creates friction, and friction creates frustration.

Bo Bennet once said, "Frustration, although quite painful at times, is a very positive and essential part of success." Seen this way, frustration is not a dead end. It is a signal.

The Three Sources of Frustration

Before frustration can be useful, it has to be understood. Most workplace friction falls into three categories:

> **Environment.** Systems, tools, or conditions make it harder to succeed. Outdated software, poor processes, or unclear policies weigh people down.
>
> **Personal.** Internal patterns, self-doubt, or unrealistic expectations create friction within.
>
> **With Others.** Miscommunication, mismatched values, or conflicting goals disrupt collaboration.

Knowing which type you are facing changes the path forward.

Turning Frustration Into Results

Once the source is clear, the next step is transformation. Frustration becomes fuel when it is used to reset expectations and redirect energy. The process is simple, but it requires honesty.

> **Identify.** Notice when you or your team are frustrated. Name it instead of burying it.
>
> **Classify.** Is this frustration environmental, personal, or with others?
>
> **Clarify.** What result was expected? What result occurred? Where is the gap?
>
> **Plan.** Identify the roadblock and outline a next step.
>
> **Communicate.** Share the goal and the plan with all invested parties.
>
> **Act.** Decide whether to change the system, shift the approach, or let go of what is only a distraction.

Step by step, frustration moves from a drain into momentum.

Story: Frustration at Home

He loaded the dishwasher quickly, satisfied to have one chore checked off. A few minutes later, she opened it to add a cup and stopped short. Bowls were stacked at odd angles, silverware clumped together. To her, it looked careless. To him, it looked done.

The gap between their expectations sat in the open door of the dishwasher.

At first, frustration rose on both sides. He felt unappreciated for helping. She felt ignored, as if her standards didn't matter. Neither one was wrong, but both were caught in the same trap , expecting one result, experiencing another.

Once the heat passed, they named it. They laughed at how two people could look at the same rack of dishes and see two different realities. He agreed to pay more attention next time. She agreed not to assume intention from the way a spoon was stacked. The dishwasher didn't become perfect, but the conversation did something better. It turned frustration into understanding.

Why It Matters

Frustration left unchecked breeds disengagement at work and disconnection at home. Frustration named and transformed builds resilience, adaptability, and trust. The skill that sets you apart is not avoiding frustration, but using it to move forward.

Reflection and Practice

1. **Notice.** Where do you feel the most frustration right now, in your environment, in yourself, or with others?

2. **Assess.** What result were you expecting that did not happen? How wide is the gap?

3. **Act.** Take one step to address it: adjust an expectation, update a system, or start one honest conversation.

The Morning and Afternoon of Life

Carl Jung once wrote, *"In the morning of life, by the afternoon I have become a lie."* He was pointing to the way we grow, how early energy and ego often carry us away from our authentic selves, and how later life asks us to return.

The Morning of Life

The morning of life is full of energy and testing. You try on identities. You chase what looks powerful. You seek out what others will approve of. This stage is marked by ambition, by the pull of ego, by the need to prove yourself.

It is not wrong. It is necessary. Just as the morning sun rises quickly and casts long shadows, this season of life is about exploration. You are discovering what you can do, even if it means stepping away from who you truly are.

The Afternoon of Life

The afternoon is different. The light shifts. Growth slows but deepens. What once looked like success begins to feel shallow if it is disconnected from meaning. The ego loosens. Wisdom gathers.

The afternoon is where love and connection matter more than trophies. It is where authenticity calls you back. In this season, the energy of the morning finds its balance, not in constant motion, but in alignment with the self.

Story: Morning and Afternoon in Career

In his twenties, Daniel was unstoppable. He climbed fast in his career, the kind of person who stayed late just to prove he could outwork everyone else. Every promotion felt like fuel. Every compliment from a boss confirmed that he mattered. He bought the car, the condo, the watch. The morning of his life was full of energy, ambition, and ego.

But by his forties, the shine had dulled. The long hours that once felt heroic began to feel hollow. Success was there on paper, but at home his marriage was strained, his children hardly knew his rhythms, and laughter felt rare. He realized that the life he had built was impressive to others but no longer true to himself.

The afternoon began with small shifts. He started leaving work on time two nights a week. He learned to cook family dinners. He picked up a paintbrush again, something he hadn't touched since high school. At first it felt clumsy, but it was his. Slowly, Daniel discovered that significance wasn't in titles or possessions, but in connection, creativity, and presence.

He had not wasted his morning. The drive and discipline he built there gave him tools. But the wisdom of the afternoon was different. It was about re-tuning to authenticity, letting go of masks, and coming back to himself.

Story: Morning and Afternoon Beyond Career

In the morning of her life, Leah wanted nothing more than to belong. She said yes to every invitation, laughed at jokes she didn't find funny, and wore clothes that never felt like her. Her circle of friends was wide, but shallow. Their approval kept her moving, even when she felt hollow inside.

By her thirties, the strain caught up. She realized most of the people around her didn't really know her. She had built connection on performance, not truth. Nights out left her tired instead of full.

The afternoon of her life began quietly. She stopped saying yes to every invitation. She started reading again, something she loved as a child but had long abandoned. She reached out to one friend she trusted and admitted she was exhausted from pretending. That conversation opened space for others that were more honest, less polished.

It was not instant. Some friendships fell away. But the ones that remained grew deeper, rooted in authenticity instead of performance. Leah found that what she once chased in crowds, she now discovered in a few steady connections.

The afternoon gave her back her own voice. What had been a lie of belonging in the morning became true connection in the afternoon.

The Arc of Return

Jung's insight reminds us that the trajectory of life is not a straight climb. The morning sends us outward, testing, stretching, building ego. The afternoon draws us inward, asking us to integrate, to return to authenticity with new wisdom.

The morning's lie is not failure. It is simply the mask you wore to survive and grow. The afternoon's work is to remove it.

Create yourself, or society will, and they don't even know you. - Anna Talyn

Reflection and Practice

1. **Notice.** Where are you right now, morning or afternoon? Are you chasing approval, or seeking alignment?

2. **Assess.** What parts of yourself feel like masks? What parts feel authentic?

3. **Act.** Choose one small way to return to your authentic self today, a word spoken honestly, a boundary held, or a connection deepened.

The Six Points of Ego

Raven often spoke about a framework she connected with through Jimmy Fannin's teachings. It names six ways the ego can disguise itself, pulling us away from authenticity and connection.

The six points of ego are:

1. **You are what you do.** Achievement becomes identity. Every success feels like proof of worth, every failure like collapse.

2. **You are what you have.** Possessions and status symbols define value. Without them, you fear being invisible.

3. **You are what people think about you.** Reputation takes center stage. Approval becomes oxygen, and disapproval feels like suffocation.

4. **Disconnected from people.** Ego isolates. Relationships are measured, guarded, and transactional.

5. **Disconnected from self.** Authentic desires are buried under roles, responsibilities, and expectations. You forget what you actually want.

6. **Disconnected from the oneness.** The larger sense of connection, to nature, spirit, or humanity itself, fades, replaced by the illusion that you are separate and alone.

Story: Ego Turned Outward

Maria lived by her résumé. Promotions gave her a rush, but when work slowed, she felt empty. She filled the gap with new clothes, a new car, new things to prove she was still moving forward. Compliments lifted her. Criticism crushed her.

At first it looked like success. But slowly she noticed her friendships thinning. Conversations became about her latest project instead of what really mattered. She laughed less. She prayed less. She felt less.

It took a long season of burnout to recognize the pattern. She wasn't her work. She wasn't her possessions. She wasn't the sum of what people said about her. The ego had disconnected her from herself, from others, and from the larger sense of belonging that had once given her peace. Naming the pattern was the first step in breaking it.

Story: Ego Turned Inward

Jon rarely worried about what others thought of him. On the outside, he looked grounded. But inside, he carried a constant sense of not measuring up. His inner voice replayed old failures like a loop: the class he dropped, the relationship that ended, the promise he hadn't kept.

He didn't need outside critics, his ego had become his own. It told him he was what he hadn't done, what he lacked, what he failed to achieve.

The disconnection grew quietly. He stopped asking what he wanted. He dismissed small joys before they had a chance to take root. He felt cut off not from the world, but from himself.

The shift began when he noticed moments of stillness, walking in the park, hearing a favorite song, cooking a simple meal. Those didn't change his résumé or reputation. But they reminded him he was more than his ego's script. He could choose to listen to the voice of enoughness instead of the voice of lack. Slowly, Jon learned that ego wasn't always about pride. Sometimes it was about forgetting your own worth.

Reflection and Practice

1. **Notice.** Which of the six points do you find yourself slipping into most often, what you do, what you have, or what others think of you?

2. **Assess.** Do you feel connected to yourself, to others, and to something larger than you, or do you feel isolated?

3. **Act.** Choose one practice this week that reconnects you, spend time with someone without performance, do one thing that has no achievement attached, or rest in silence until you hear your own voice again.

The Connections

Love is not just poetry and promise. It is also chemistry. Our bodies are designed to bond, and the brain plays its part by releasing a small orchestra of chemicals that shape attraction, intimacy, and attachment.

The Chemistry of Love

- **Dopamine.** The spark of excitement. This is the chemical of reward and anticipation, the rush you feel when you see someone you desire or achieve a goal you've longed for.

- **Oxytocin.** The bonding chemical. Often called the "cuddle hormone," oxytocin builds trust, calms the nervous system, and deepens emotional connection.

- **Vasopressin.** The commitment chemical. It plays a role in long-term attachment and loyalty, turning attraction into steadiness.

- **Serotonin.** The mood stabilizer. It shapes well-being and even colors how attractive someone appears to us, reinforcing the bond through feeling good in their presence.

These chemicals don't dictate love, but they do frame how we experience it. Biology gives us the tools; choice and intention give them direction.

Lessons from Nature

Bonding is not the same for every creature. A baby chicken needs a parent for only about a week before it can survive on its own. A frog needs no parenting at all. But humans are different. We are complex, social organisms, and it takes fourteen or more years for a child to learn how to live in the world.

That long season of dependency reveals something profound: love is not just about reproduction or survival. It is about teaching, shaping, and carrying forward a way of life. We are built to stay connected for the long haul.

Levels of Relationship

Not all relationships function at the same level. They move through stages, and sometimes they get stuck.

> **All About Me.** At this stage, the focus is selfish. Love is defined by what it gives you, not what it builds together.
> **Horse Trading.** Here, love becomes bargaining. "If you do this, I'll do that." It is conditional, measured, and often fragile.
> **Unconditional Love.** This is love from overflow. You are already complete, and so your giving is not about filling a lack but about sharing abundance.
> **Gandhi / Mandela Love.** At the highest level, love transcends individual bonds. It becomes a force for justice, forgiveness, and change. This is love as a collective power.

Story: From Bargaining to Overflow

When they first moved in together, their arguments often circled back to chores. She would say, "I did the laundry, so you should do the dishes." He would reply, "I took out the trash, so why can't you handle dinner?" It was always a balance sheet. Every act of care carried a tally mark.

At times it worked. The house stayed clean, meals got made. But underneath, something felt thin. Their love had started to sound like transactions, each one negotiated.

The shift came after a long week when everything went wrong, the car broke down, work piled up, and both of them were exhausted. She came home one night to find dinner already made. He had done it without asking for credit or expecting trade. When she thanked him, he shrugged and said, "I just wanted you to rest."

That small moment broke the pattern. The dishes and laundry still mattered, but they began to see love not as horse trading, but as overflow. Acts of care became gifts, not bargains.

They didn't abandon responsibility. They still divided chores. But the energy changed. Each action came from fullness, not from a need to keep score. In that shift, they discovered that love grows deepest when it flows freely.

Reflection and Practice

1. **Notice.** Which chemical of love do you most recognize in your current or past relationships, dopamine, oxytocin, vasopressin, or serotonin?

2. **Assess.** Where would you place most of your relationships on the spectrum, selfish, bargaining, unconditional, or transcendent?

3. **Act.** Choose one practice this week to lift a relationship one level higher, replace a bargain with a gift, or a moment of selfishness with a choice to connect.

Sacrifice vs. Giving

and the Trap of Conflict Avoidance

Sacrifice and giving may look the same on the outside, but the difference underneath changes everything.

Sacrifice comes from depletion. It is when you give what you do not have, hoping it will be enough. Over time, sacrifice turns to resentment. Resentment hardens into distance. What began as love can quietly corrode into bitterness.

Conflict avoidance works the same way. You swallow your feelings to keep the peace. You nod when you want to disagree. You say "it's fine" when it isn't. At first, it feels like the loving thing to do. You tell yourself you are protecting them from hurt or shielding them from extra burden. And in the beginning, the intention is good. But silence accumulates. Each avoided conversation becomes another weight you carry alone. Over time, that quiet pile of resentment can turn even happy marriages into cold partnerships, even friendships into distance.

Giving, on the other hand, comes from overflow. Speaking the truth, even gently, comes from overflow too. Both require that you are steady enough to be honest, rested enough to set a boundary, and safe enough to express yourself. Overflow multiplies. Sacrifice and avoidance deplete.

Story: When Silence Becomes Resentment

Maya hated arguments, so she rarely spoke up when something bothered her. If her partner left dishes in the sink, she just cleaned them. If he forgot to call, she brushed it off. "It's not worth fighting over," she told herself.

Her reasoning came from love. She didn't want to nag, didn't want to hurt his feelings, didn't want to seem ungrateful. But inside, each silence left a mark. She started to feel unseen, unvalued. Small slights grew in her mind until even neutral words sounded sharp. After years of avoiding conflict, she no longer felt close to him. Love had been slowly replaced by resentment.

The change came only when she dared to speak. The first conversations were messy, but honest. She realized that avoiding conflict hadn't kept peace, it had built walls. Speaking up began to tear them down.

Story: Overflow in Action

Anna once believed love meant self-sacrifice. She said yes to every request, stayed up late to finish what others left undone, gave even when her body and mind were empty. At first, people praised her. She looked dependable. But inside, she felt brittle.

The turning point came when she began to treat her own well-being as part of the equation. She slept more. She said no when she needed to. She set boundaries. Slowly, her energy returned.

The surprising part was that when she started giving again, it felt lighter. Cooking dinner for her kids became joy, not duty. Helping a friend felt like connection, not obligation. The love she shared wasn't reduced by self-care. It was multiplied.

Living From Overflow

Overflow is not indulgence. It is wisdom. It recognizes that if the cup is empty, no one benefits. But if the cup is full and spilling over, giving is natural, honest, and sustaining.

Conflict avoidance often begins with good intentions, but unspoken truths eventually erode trust. Sacrifice may feel noble at first, but emptiness eventually breeds resentment. The real work is to fill first, then speak, then give. That rhythm sustains connection instead of breaking it.

The Chemistry Behind It

Our bodies tell the story as clearly as our relationships do.

- **Sacrifice and silence** build stress. When needs are denied or words swallowed, cortisol, the body's stress hormone, rises. Over time, chronic cortisol wears down patience, empathy, and health.

- **Overflow and honesty** release oxytocin. Acts of genuine giving and truthful connection build trust and ease tension. Instead of draining you, they calm the body and deepen the bond.

What feels heavy or light is not only emotional. It is physiological. Your body knows when you are empty and when you are full.

Reflection and Practice

1. **Notice.** Do you tend to give from emptiness, or avoid conflict to keep peace?

2. **Assess.** How have those patterns affected your relationships , have small silences built into resentment?

3. **Act.** Choose one small boundary to honor this week, or one honest conversation to have, and see how it changes the energy.

Emotions

Emotions are not weaknesses to be hidden. They are guides, signals, and often the very energy that moves us. Possibility takes movement, and movement takes emotion.

Fear Is Different Than What We Were Told

Fear is often painted as the enemy, something to be overcome or eliminated. But fear has two faces, and each serves a purpose.

> **Fear of the current situation.** This is the survival instinct, the fear that alerts you to real danger in the moment. It keeps you alive.
>
> **Fear of the unknown.** This is the fear of change, of not knowing what happens next.

It's important to be clear: we are not suggesting that every fear of the unknown is safe or should be ignored. Outside of a reflective or evaluative environment, fear may signal risk you need to respect. Here, we are focusing on the fear that rises when you consider stepping into growth, taking a risk that stretches you. That fear does not mean danger. It means you are moving beyond the familiar.

When you learn to distinguish between these two, fear stops being an obstacle. It becomes a guidepost. The path of growth is often uncomfortable, but that discomfort is not a stop sign. It is a signal that you are on ground where good things can happen.

How Emotions Feel in the Body

Emotions do not live only in the mind. Anxiety can tighten your chest. Sadness can feel like weight in your stomach. Gratitude can ease your muscles. Joy can quicken your breath.

You cannot simply stop emotions. They rise automatically, a function of being human. But you can learn to notice them, to listen to what they are saying, and to decide what to do with the energy they create.

The Emotions Light Switch

When emotions feel overwhelming, clarity can be found in separating what is feeling from what is fact. Imagine a light switch. On one side is the full flood of emotion - intense, clouding, heavy. On the other side is logic - the bare outline of what is happening, without story or judgment.

The practice begins by noticing the edges of your emotions. Feel where the raw sensation of emotion ends and the hard lines of fact begin. These register differently in your mind. Emotions often feel heavy, buzzing, or restless. Facts feel cooler and steadier. Learning to observe that difference helps your brain categorize what you are experiencing.

Here's how the practice works step by step:

1. **Feel for the edges.** Ask yourself: which parts of this are emotions, and which parts are facts? Notice the different "textures" of each.

2. **Switch to logic.** Lay out only the facts of the situation - what happened, what was said, what is objectively true.

3. **Imagine outcomes.** From this logical base, ask yourself what outcome you would want if the situation unfolded perfectly. Identify the actions that would move you toward it.

4. **Switch back to emotion.** Invite the emotions back in. Turn back on the Emotions Light Switch. Let them illuminate the situation more fully. Notice how they change your view of the facts and your imagined outcomes. Do they affirm the path, or highlight something you overlooked?

5. **Check the body.** If emotions still feel unclear, observe physical cues: tense shoulders, a tight stomach, shallow breathing. Work upward -tension in the body → anxiety → fear of the unknown. Then ask, *what possibility might exist in that unknown?*

6. **Integrate.** Bring body, mind, and heart together. Facts give clarity. Emotions give depth and guidance. Together, they create the fullest picture.

7. **Decide and act.** Once logic and emotion are aligned, choose your next step and move into action.

Logic alone cannot reveal the best outcome. Emotions alone cannot either. But separated, then recombined, they illuminate the path. That illumination is what gives The Emotions *Light Switch* its name.

Story: Using the Light Switch

Carla sat at her desk long after her shift had ended, staring at an unopened email from her manager. The subject line read: *Meeting Request*. Her chest was tight, her stomach knotted. A dozen thoughts raced through her mind. Did *I do something wrong? Am I about to be fired?*

The emotions felt like a flood, so she tried the Light Switch method.

First, she paused and felt for the edges. The pounding heart, the tight stomach, that was anxiety. The fear underneath was the fear of the unknown.

Then she flipped to logic. Fact: she had received an email asking for a meeting. Fact: there was no mention of discipline. Fact: her performance reviews had been positive.

From there, she asked herself: what outcome would I want if this were a perfect situation? She imagined the meeting as a chance to discuss a project she cared about, or even a new opportunity.

Then she brought emotions back in. Her fear reminded her she valued stability. But her hope reminded her she wanted growth. Both were true, and both mattered.

Finally, she checked her body again. When she pictured speaking honestly in the meeting, asking if there was an opportunity to grow, her shoulders eased a little. That was the signal. Her body, mind, and heart were pointing in the same direction.

By the time she closed her laptop, the decision was clear. She would show up to the meeting prepared, open, and willing to hear the truth. The fear had not vanished, but it had turned into a guidepost instead of a wall.

Emotions as Decision Makers

Every major decision carries emotion. You do not move toward possibility with facts alone. Emotions are the spark that make action possible. Even hesitation is movement, a choice not to act.

The goal is not to silence emotions or to let them run wild. The goal is to notice them, work with them, and use their energy to create change that matters.

Reflection and Practice

1. **Notice.** What emotion do you feel most often in your body - anxiety, joy, sadness, gratitude? Where does it show up?

2. **Assess.** When you feel fear, is it fear for your safety in the present, or fear of the unknown that points to change?

3. **Act.** Try the Emotions Light Switch method with one current stressor. Separate facts from feelings, then add them back together to guide your next step.

4. **Observe.** The next time your body tenses, pause and trace it upward: body → emotion → meaning. What guidepost is the emotion pointing to?

5. **Experiment.** Pick one situation this week where you normally avoid acting because of emotion. Instead of resisting, lean into it. See what possibility shows up in the discomfort.

6. **Reflect.** Ask yourself: are my emotions controlling me, or am I learning to work with them? Write down one example of each from your recent life.

Dreams

Dreams are not random noise. They are built from feelings. The brain senses an emotion, fear, joy, longing, and then works backward, filling in images and storylines that match. That is why dreams can feel vivid but strange, both true and surreal at once.

Raven often said, *"You should always be the hero, and it should always work out."* She believed that even in dreams, the self deserves a space where things resolve, where courage shows up, where possibility wins.

When you dream from fear alone, the stories can spiral into nightmares. But when you dream with the belief that you can overcome, the dream becomes a rehearsal space for possibility. It is practice for the waking world.

Dreams are not predictions. They are reflections of what your body and mind are carrying. Pay attention to the feelings behind them. Ask: *What emotion started this dream? What might it be pointing toward in my waking life?*

Reflection and Practice

1. **Notice.** Think of a dream you've had recently. Instead of the images, focus on the feeling that began it. Was it fear, hope, loss, desire?

2. **Reframe.** When you find yourself in a dream, or remembering one, ask: *How would this look if I were the hero and it worked out?*

3. **Apply.** Take that reframed ending and bring it into waking life. What would it look like to carry that same courage or resolution into your next real challenge?

High Performance Habits

Raven was a huge believer in Brendon Burchard's *High Performance Habits*. She studied his work closely and used it as a guide for her own life. The six habits he identified, clarity, energy, necessity, productivity, influence, and courage, became a kind of anchor for her. They're not ours to reinvent, but they shaped so much of how Raven lived and taught that leaving them out would be a gap.

If you want the full depth, Brendon's book is the place to go. What follows here are glimpses of how Raven lived these habits in her daily life, and how I've seen them create possibility in mine too.

Seek Clarity

Clarity is about knowing what matters most and keeping it in view. Raven kept notes where she would see it everyday, a constant reminder of what she was working toward. She didn't let clarity become complicated, she kept the important things visible, top of mind, and in motion.

Generate Energy

Energy isn't luck. It's cultivated. Raven would juice in the mornings to fuel her body and break big goals into small, efficient steps. She had a way of turning everything into numbers, making the path concrete and manageable. That structure gave her energy because it replaced overwhelm with action.

Raise Necessity

Necessity is about tying goals to purpose. For Raven, that meant putting others first. She cared deeply about how her choices affected the people around her. That sense of responsibility was not a burden, it gave her direction. She lived like showing up well was never optional, because someone always needed her best.

Increase Productivity

Productivity is often confused with multitasking. Raven lived it differently. She could focus deeply on a few things at once , whether it was piano, singing, or sports , and give her full attention until the goal was met. Her productivity was never just about achievement; it was also about finding ways to make progress while still keeping space for others.

Develop Influence

Influence grows from listening, and Raven excelled at it. She didn't just hear words; she listened with her full heart. People left conversations with her feeling known and valued. That was her influence, not titles or authority, but the ability to connect so deeply that people wanted to rise higher simply by being near her.

Demonstrate Courage

Courage is the moment when thinking gives way to action. Raven and I both knew the weight of that. We took leaps we were not ready for, scared and worried, but knowing that growth never happens in the safe zone. Possibility takes movement, and sometimes the only way through is to stop circling the "what ifs" and step forward anyway.

Reflection and Practice

1. **Clarity.** Write down one goal and put it somewhere you'll see every day this week.

2. **Energy.** Break a big task into the smallest possible step and complete it today.

3. **Necessity.** Ask yourself: who benefits when I show up as my best?

4. **Productivity.** Choose three things that matter most tomorrow, and let go of the rest.

5. **Influence.** Listen to someone without distraction, without planning your reply, just to understand.

6. **Courage.** Take one step you've been avoiding because of fear. Even if small, do it today.

Reprogramming the Junk

We are born with momentum. A child doesn't need to be told to grow, to explore, to laugh. The energy is already there, a kind of perpetual motion machine that gathers inertia with every step.

But as we grow, layers of programming begin to shape us. Some are meant to protect: *eat on a schedule, look both ways, follow the rules.* Others come from culture and family: *clean your plate, sit still in church, boys don't wear pink, girls don't play rough.* Over time, these ideas accumulate. Some keep us safe. Others begin to shrink us.

Not all programming is spoken outright. Sometimes it comes as jokes, taunts, or throwaway phrases that stick deeper than anyone intended:

- *You're not good enough.*
- *You'll never amount to anything.*
- *You're stupid.*
- *That's for boys, not girls.*
- *You're too much.*
- *You're not enough.*

They echo long after childhood, shaping the way we see ourselves and what we believe is possible.

Story: The Pink Jump Rope

On the playground one afternoon, a boy reached for the only jump rope left in the pile. It happened to be pink. The moment his hand closed around it, another kid laughed and shouted, "That's a girl's rope! You can't use that."

He froze. The rope hadn't been heavy until that moment, but now it felt impossible to lift. The game went on without him.

It wasn't about the rope. It was about the message that slid in quietly: *pink is off limits, certain choices are off limits, you are wrong for even trying.*

He wasn't allergic to the rope. But the programming landed like one. From then on, he avoided pink, avoided anything that might draw the same reaction. A single moment reshaped what he thought was allowed.

Years later, he thought back to that day. He realized it had never been about the rope at all, it was about permission. And permission was something he could give himself.

So he tried again. Not with a jump rope this time, but in other choices that once felt off limits. He bought a shirt in a color he had avoided. He spoke an opinion he once held back. He let himself be seen in ways he had once hidden.

Each small act was a rewrite. The old message said, *you can't.* The new message said, *I can, if I choose to.*

This is how we reprogram the junk. We notice where the old scripts came from, we decide whether they serve us, and we write new ones that do. The rope was never the problem. The message was. And messages can change.

The truth is this: you are not alone in carrying these old scripts. We all have them. And they are not the truth of who you are.

You are enough. You are a child of the universe, made of stars, and worthy to shine among them. The work is not to erase your past, but to reprogram the junk. To notice the beliefs that hold you back, decide whether they serve you, and replace them with ones that lift instead of diminish.

This doesn't mean rejecting every structure. Some routines and rules still help. But the difference is choice. When you choose what to carry forward and what to set down, you reclaim the momentum you were born with.

Reflection and Practice

1. **Notice.** Write down three old phrases or "rules" you heard growing up that still echo in your head.

2. **Assess.** Ask: do these beliefs serve me, or do they shrink me?

3. **Reprogram.** Replace each one with a truth you choose. For example, change *"I'm not good enough"* into *"I am enough, and I am still growing."*

4. **Affirm.** Each time the old script surfaces, speak the new one out loud. Repetition builds the new program.

Nutrition and Movement

For Raven, nutrition was not a side note. It was a foundation. She often said she wished she had found this wisdom earlier in life. Once she did discover it, she lived it fully and encouraged others to do the same.

Much of her thinking was influenced by Dr. Joel Fuhrman's work, along with other nutritional researchers. Their core message: food is not just fuel for the moment. It is information for your cells, shaping how your body repairs, resists, and grows.

Nutrition for High Performance

An alkaline state in the body helps remove and prevent the build-up of acids that contribute to degenerative conditions. Live, nutrient-dense foods deliver energy to your cells that goes far beyond the quick spikes of processed sugar or refined grains.

Our taste buds evolved in a world where food was scarce. Sweetness and fat meant survival. Today, that same programming often works against us. Foods engineered for pleasure can overwhelm our palate and steer us away from what the body truly needs.

Raven's Practice

Raven followed Dr. Fuhrman's recommendation to eat the largest salad you can manage about an hour before dinner. To her, it was more than a tip, it was a daily ritual. That plate of greens, vegetables, nuts, and seeds "preloaded" her body with what it needed most. Whatever came after, her cells had already received the nutrients to carry her forward.

She saw firsthand that shifting one meal or one habit at a time could change energy, focus, and mood.

Changing Guidelines

When Raven was young, the food pyramid was built on wheat at the base, then dairy stacked above it. Today, we see epidemics of diabetes, heart disease, and other chronic conditions linked to those very foods. What we once thought of as foundational has proven, for many, to be harmful in excess.

This is why questioning old programming, even in nutrition, matters. We cannot assume that what we were taught as children is what our bodies need for health today.

Beneficial Bacteria

Gut health also changes with age. By the time many people reach fifty, much of the beneficial bacteria that once supported digestion and immunity has diminished. Paying attention to probiotics, fiber, and foods that support healthy bacteria is part of restoring balance.

Movement and Nature

Nutrition is only one side of the equation. Movement completes it. Exercise does not have to be extreme to be effective. Raven valued simply getting outside, connecting with the earth, walking, moving, reminding the body that it was designed for rhythm and flow.

Movement clears the mind, releases stress, and supports the very systems that nutrition feeds.

Resources

For readers who want to go deeper, Raven recommended:

Dr. Joel Fuhrman – for nutrition grounded in cellular health.

Dr. Robert Barefoot – for insights on alkalinity and prevention.

Reflection and Practice

1. **Notice.** What part of your daily eating feels most depleting? Most energizing?

2. **Shift.** Add one live, nutrient-rich food to your meals this week.

3. **Try.** Experiment with the "largest salad before dinner" ritual and see how your body responds.

4. **Move.** Get outside at least once a day, even for a short walk. Let nature reset your system.

5. **Question.** Revisit one "rule" about food you grew up with. Does it still serve you, or is it time to rewrite it?

The Lifecycle of Learning and Growth

Raven often described human development as a series of spinning vortices , each stage of growth carrying its own rhythm, energy, and way of processing the world.

Brainwave States and Early Growth

From the last trimester of pregnancy until about age two, children live primarily in the **delta** state, the slowest brainwave rhythm. This is a stage of absorption, where the body grows rapidly and the mind begins to imprint its first patterns.

Between ages two and six, the brain shifts to **theta**. In this stage, imagination rules. Children play, create, and believe almost anything is possible. It is also the window when messages about identity, worth, and limits sink deepest, because the conscious filters are not yet built.

From ages six to twelve, **alpha** waves dominate. The mind begins to balance imagination with structure. Kids start to test rules, form strategies, and carry ideas from play into more concrete plans.

By twelve and onward, **beta** becomes the default. This is the state of analysis, focus, and judgment. The mind sharpens, but it can also narrow. Possibility becomes easier to doubt.

By the time a person reaches about **eighteen**, they are "reared", equipped with the mental tools needed to survive. For animals, this rearing age multiplied by seven roughly predicts lifespan. By that measure, humans would live into their 120s. In reality, most live far fewer years. The gap is not just biology, it reflects how we live, what we eat, how we move, and how we respond to stress.

The Retreat of Early Benefits

The qualities we carry as children, openness, curiosity, the ability to absorb with ease, often retreat as we age. The imagination of theta and the openness of alpha give way to the busyness of beta. We trade wonder for analysis, possibility for certainty.

Yet those earlier gifts are not lost. They can be revisited. Meditation, play, rest, and intentional learning can reawaken the slower, more open states of the mind. The vortex keeps spinning, but we can shift its rhythm.

The Next Levels

If rearing is the first major threshold, what comes after? The answer is not fixed. For some, it feels like expansion, returning to imagination, wisdom, and connection. For others, it feels like contraction, clinging to certainty and resisting change.

The invitation is this: notice the rhythm of the stage you are in. Are you in the slow openness of delta, the imagination of theta, the balance of alpha, or the judgment of beta? Each state has value. Each can be revisited, practiced, and integrated.

The question is not how long we live. The question is how fully we move through the levels available to us, and what possibilities we allow ourselves to see along the way.

Reprogramming the Brain

Our brains are built for efficiency. They create shortcuts, labels, and default patterns so we can move through the world quickly. These patterns often keep us safe, but they also keep us stuck.

Removing Memes and Labels

Labels are quick categories the brain uses to reduce complexity. They can be useful ("hot stove, don't touch") but also limiting ("boys don't cry," "I'm not good at math"). Over time, these labels become memes, repeated stories we tell ourselves and each other until they feel like truth.

The first step toward possibility is noticing the labels. Which ones were handed to you? Which ones have you repeated so often they feel permanent? Once you notice them, you can choose whether to keep or rewrite them.

The Three Residents of the Brain

Think of the brain as having three primary "residents":

> **Back brain.** The survival center, focused on safety and fight-or-flight responses.
>
> **Mid brain.** The emotional center, where feelings and connections are processed.
>
> **Front brain.** The reasoning center, capable of reflection, planning, and conscious choice.

Most of our unhelpful programming sits deep in the back and mid brain. To reprogram, we have to help the front brain communicate without triggering automatic defenses.

Story: Remapping Fish

For years, I had an aversion to fish and seafood. It wasn't based on logic or even experience , just a reaction that didn't make sense to me. I decided it didn't serve me anymore, especially since it disrupted meals with others who enjoyed it.

So I began to reprogram. Each time I encountered fish, I gave my brain a new message it could accept. At first it was simple: *this is healthy food, and others love it*. Over time I strengthened the messaging: *this doesn't smell bad, this could be delicious, I might be missing out*.

Eventually, I started to think about fish when I was hungry. I told myself: *fish would be delicious to try*. I ordered it, and kept practicing.

It took a couple of years, but the change held. Fish is still not my favorite, but I now enjoy it, and even some seafood and sushi. The key was catching the brain in the moment of reaction and swapping in a new message at a level it would accept. Bit by bit, I remapped my brain from aversion to tolerance, and finally to enjoyment.

This same process can work with childhood messages, old fears, or limiting beliefs. Reprogramming is possible.

Four Ways to Reprogram

Research and practice show at least four reliable methods for rewriting brain patterns:

1. **Habituation.** Repetition creates new grooves. The more you repeat a message or behavior, the more the brain adopts it as normal.

2. **Hypnosis.** In theta states, whether in deep relaxation, meditation, or the edge of sleep, the brain is more open to suggestion and change.

3. **Energy psychology.** Techniques that calm the nervous system can allow the front brain to communicate with the back without triggering fight-or-flight.

4. **High-impact events.** Trauma can reprogram instantly, but so can powerful positive experiences. A decision tied to a strong emotional event can reshape patterns quickly.

Confusion is another doorway. When the brain doesn't know how to respond, it pauses. In that pause, you have a chance to define the reaction yourself instead of letting society or old scripts define it for you.

Memory Pegs

A memory peg is an anchor point, a lighthouse you can return to when you need grounding. It might be a phrase, a place, or even a small physical act. The peg reminds you of who you are becoming and helps steady you when old patterns resurface.

Creating Behavior

The most important truth is this: you can create behavior. You are not locked into the one created for you in youth, in trauma, or by culture. Awareness opens the door. Practice walks you through it. Choice makes it your own.

Reflection and Practice

1. **Spot the label.** Write down one phrase or belief that still echoes from childhood or past experience. Example: *I'm not good at public speaking.*

2. **Catch the reaction.** The next time the belief shows up, pause and notice where you feel it in your body , tight chest, shallow breath, stomach drop. Naming the reaction slows the loop.

3. **Swap the message.** Offer your brain a new statement it can accept. Start simple: *This is just practice,* or *I can improve.* Over time, build toward stronger affirmations: *I have a voice worth hearing.*

4. **Use habituation.** Repeat the new message in small, consistent ways. Say it out loud, write it down, or pair it with an action like standing tall or taking a deep breath.

5. **Create a memory peg.** Choose one anchor , a phrase, a touchstone, a small ritual , that reminds you of the new message. Use it whenever you feel the old program rising.

6. **Lean into confusion.** When you don't know what to do, pause before defaulting. In that moment, ask: *What choice would serve who I am becoming, not just who I've been?*

Closing Reflections

Possibility is not one moment of inspiration. It is a progression. We move through levels, each one shaping us in a different way.

The first level is **good information**. You read, you listen, you learn something new. It feels exciting, like beginner's luck. In this stage, you feel like you've got it. But when life presses back, the ideas don't always hold. Knowledge alone can't carry you through the test.

The second level is **choice**. You start to practice. You stumble. You face the gap between what you know and how you live. This is where frustration often rises, but also where learning deepens. It takes two, sometimes three rounds through this cycle before the lessons hold.

The third level is **knowing**. This is more than thought. It is when the lesson sinks past theory into lived truth. You don't have to remind yourself, it has become part of you. It is not that struggle disappears, but that you trust yourself to move through it.

You can call these planes, tiers, stages, alignments. The names don't matter. What matters is remembering that each level is necessary. Information opens the door. Choice teaches resilience. Knowing anchors you in possibility.

Wherever you are in this cycle, you are not behind. You are in process. And process is where possibility lives.

Possibility is not waiting at the far end of the road. It is here, in the choice you make next. Every step you've taken in reading this book has been its own act of movement, its own proof that you are open to growth.

Raven believed deeply in this work. She lived it, taught it, and wished she had found some of these truths earlier in her own journey. Her voice is woven through these pages as both reminder and invitation: you are not alone, you are not behind, and you are capable of more than you have been told.

I thank you for walking with us through these ideas, through the frameworks, the stories, the reflections. The real change comes not from finishing this book, but from carrying its questions into your daily life.

So keep listening to your body. Keep noticing the signals. Keep practicing the small steps that move you forward. When fear rises, remember it may be pointing to growth. When old scripts echo, remember they can be rewritten. And when possibility feels far away, remember it is already here.

You are enough. You are worthy to shine. And you have everything you need to step into your own possibility of happy.

Practical Recap / Quick Guide

These are not prescriptions. They are starting points, simple anchors you can return to when life feels overwhelming or when you need a reminder of where possibility lives.

Notice signals. Your body and emotions are not distractions; they are guides. Listen for hunger, tension, fatigue, joy.

Honor the pillars. Stability matters. Keep routines or supports that ground you, even as you build new habits.

Reprogram the junk. Old labels and messages are not permanent. Replace them with truths you choose.

Choose movement. Possibility grows with action, even in small steps.

Anchor your why. Connect goals to purpose, who and what matter most.

Fuel your body. Live foods, balanced energy, and movement in nature create the foundation for change.

Practice the Light Switch. Separate fact from feeling, then bring them together to illuminate the way forward.

Lean into fear. Distinguish survival fear from growth fear. One protects; the other points to possibility.

Rewrite endings. In dreams, in thoughts, in life: see yourself as the hero, and let it work out.

Return to knowing. Growth cycles from information, to choice, to lived truth. Trust the process.

Keep this page close. When the world feels complicated, come back to these simple cues. They are reminders that you already carry the capacity for change, and that the possibility of happy is not somewhere else. It is here, with you.

Acknowledgments

This book is not the work of one person. It is the result of voices, lessons, and love woven together across years.

First, to Raven McGee, my co-author, my friend, and the heart of this work. Raven lived the principles in these pages with conviction and courage. She believed in possibility even when life pressed hard against her. Her wisdom, humor, and presence continue to echo here. Though she is no longer with us, her voice is part of every chapter.

To Raven's spouse, thank you for encouraging me to carry this forward. Your trust and generosity made it possible to bring Raven's contributions into the world so others could learn from them.

To my family, thank you for giving me space and support to write. For the steady love and acceptance that reminded me why possibility matters, and for keeping me grounded when the work felt heavy.

To the friends, colleagues, and workshop participants who shared stories, asked questions, and reminded us that this work is not abstract but lived, thank you. Your voices helped shape these pages more than you know.

And to you, the reader, thank you for choosing possibility. You are part of this circle now. May you carry forward your own possibility of happy and make it real in ways only you can.

Closing Note

This book grew out of years of conversations, workshops, and lived experiments. When the two of us met, we were already carrying our own ideas about growth, change, and possibility. What surprised us was how seamlessly those ideas overlapped, how theories we had tested in different corners of life seemed to fit together as if they had been waiting to meet.

Raven was the most selfless person you could encounter. She had a way of changing lives in the smallest moments. Even standing in line at the grocery store, she would ask someone how they were, pause at the first polite answer, and gently ask again, *but how are you really?* She gave that level of attention to every human she crossed paths with.

Though she is no longer here, her presence remains. Through her words and her work, we hope her influence continues to ripple outward, changing the world one conversation, one insight, one act of courage at a time.

With gratitude,
Anna Talyn

For Raven

www.ingramcontent.com/pod-product-compliance
Lightning Source LLC
Chambersburg PA
CBHW070623050426
42450CB00011B/3111